Learning About Virtues

A Guide to Making Good Choices

Written by Juliette Garesché
Illustrated by R.W. Alley

ONE
CARING
PLACE

Abbey Press
St. Meinrad, IN 47577

This book is dedicated to all children in hopes
that via virtue they may find peace.

Text © 2009 Juliette Garesché Dages
Illustrations © 2009 Saint Meinrad Archabbey
Published by One Caring Place
Abbey Press
St. Meinrad, Indiana 47577

Library of Congress Catalog Number
2008943873

ISBN 978-0-87029-420-4

Printed in the United States of America

A Message to Parents, Teachers, and Other Caring Adults

You are in a unique position to teach children about virtues—positive attitudes in guiding our actions to reflect God's goodness according to reason and faith. When we model good behavior for our children, we are teaching them how to build the habit of practicing virtue.

This book introduces the concept and basic vocabulary of virtues. It helps children to recognize and label the behaviors which they are striving to develop.

God, the source of infinite goodness and love, beckons us to learn about virtues, to become virtuous. "Be holy, for I, the Lord, your God, am holy," Scripture tells us. (Leviticus 19:2) "Whatever is true, whatever is honorable, whatever is just, whatever is pure, whatever is lovely, whatever is gracious, if there is any excellence, if there is anything worthy of praise, think about these things." (Philippians 4:8)

These good things are in each of us, since we are created in God's image; but, we must exercise our will in putting them to work in our lives. In other words, we must make the *choice* to be virtuous, to do what is right in God's eyes. This requires faith, knowledge, practice, hard work, and commitment.

Young children are likely to attain one virtue at a time. The more mature the individual, the more discipline he or she may exercise in choosing words or deeds that exemplify the virtues they have learned. When a child attains a virtue, that trait will become almost habitual for them.

It isn't always easy. Life produces many challenges, and today's culture often seems to oppose virtue. However, through faith, humanity's best traits are revealed when responding to a challenging situation. Virtuous people know what Scripture confirms: "Suffering produces endurance, and endurance produces character." (Romans 5:3-4) Through a lifetime of meeting such challenges, practicing virtue, and building character, a child grows through adulthood, planting more seeds of God's goodness along the way.

We hope you have fun introducing virtues to the children in your life. This book is just the start. Be creative, and don't forget to catch your children being good! Praise their every effort toward goodness and God-likeness.

—Juliette Garesché Dages

Honest

Hector is <u>honest</u>.

Hector was hitting baseballs when a foul ball broke a neighbor's window. Hector felt horrible. He didn't want to admit he had broken the window, but he knew it was the right thing to do.

Hector worked up the courage to ring the neighbor's doorbell. When his neighbor came to the door, Hector explained what happened, and apologized. To pay for the window, Hector agreed to rake leaves for his neighbor.

Hector was **honest**, even though he was worried about what might happen. Hector had to pay for the damage, but his conscience was clear because he told the truth.

What is one way you can practice being <u>honest</u>?

Responsible

Reynaldo is <u>responsible</u>.

As a young boy, Reynaldo had many friends in school. As he got older, some of his friends began getting into trouble. Sometimes, the boys dared one another to do things—usually things the boys knew were wrong, or things for which they knew their parents would disapprove.

Reynaldo was **responsible** and had a good sense of right and wrong. He was able to make good choices, and to select friends and have fun without breaking rules. Reynaldo and his friends had harmless fun and were sometimes downright silly, but didn't get into serious trouble.

What is one way you can practice being <u>responsible</u>?

Just

Jillian is <u>just</u>.

Jillian went to watch her little sister play soccer. The players and coaches were there, but the referee didn't show up. The coaches asked Jillian if she would referee the game, and she agreed.

When Jillian had to make a decision about which team hit the ball out of bounds, or if a player had used her hands, she had to be fair. She could not give any preference to her sister's team. Jillian was **just** and fair in making her decisions. She treated both teams equally.

What is one way you can practice being <u>just</u>?

Courageous

Carl is <u>courageous</u>.

Carl was at the park with his friend Cody. A bigger boy came over and began to tease and then push Cody.

Carl stayed at Cody's side and told the bigger boy to leave his friend alone. When the boy threatened to beat up Carl, he called to other children at the park to help him.

When five children faced the boy, he said something mean and walked away. Carl was **courageous** because he continued to do the right thing even when it was difficult or scary.

What is one way you can practice being <u>*courageous*</u>*?*

Self-Controlled

Suzanne is <u>self-controlled</u>.

Suzanne was enjoying the playground swing during recess. Suddenly, a boy pushed her so hard she fell out of the swing. Though surprised, Suzanne stood up and asked the boy why he had done that. The boy said he was sorry, and explained that he had thought she was his sister, Sadie, who liked to be pushed high on the swing.

The boy pointed out his sister, and from the back she did look like Suzanne. Suzanne was **self-controlled** because instead of getting angry, she asked the boy to explain his action. The boy introduced Suzanne to Sadie. They laughed about the mistake, and became good friends.

What is one way you can practice being <u>self-controlled</u>?

Faithful

Francesca is <u>faithful</u>.

Francesca used to be afraid to go into the basement. She didn't really know why. But once her brother had accidentally turned off the lights and closed the door at the top of the stairs. Her imagination quickly filled with all sorts of scary ideas.

Francesca's mother told her not to be afraid. She said God is everywhere—even in the basement—and always watches over her. That made Francesca feel better. Francesca is **faithful** because now when she gets nervous or becomes afraid, she remembers that God is with her.

What is one way you can practice being <u>faithful</u>?

Prayerful

Patty is <u>prayerful</u>.

Ever since she was little, Patty has watched her parents do the same thing each morning. They pour a cup of coffee, and then sit at the kitchen table to give thanks and ask God to help them through the day. Her mother and father take turns reading a quote from the Bible, a short story, and a brief prayer.

Patty is now old enough to read, and joins her parents for the family prayer time in the morning. By praying with her parents and also on her own, Patty has become closer to God. She is **prayerful** throughout the day, asking for God to help her always do what is right.

What is one way you can practice being <u>prayerful</u>?

Charitable

Chad is <u>charitable</u>.

Chad's classmates were getting ready to elect a class president. Several students wanted to be elected.

Chad was always doing kind things for other people. When one of his classmates had trouble with subtraction, Chad volunteered to stay in from recess to help her study. If a classmate forgot his lunch, Chad offered to share his own lunch.

Chad is **charitable** because he is willing to give what he has to help others—whether it is his lunch, his time, or a kind word. For this reason, Chad's classmates elected him to be their class president.

What is one way you can practice being <u>charitable</u>?

Joyful

John is <u>joyful</u>.

John was about to turn 10 years old. His parents wanted to have a birthday party, but his father had lost his job, and they didn't have much money.

On the morning of his birthday, John was excited. His mother packed a picnic lunch, and they all went to the beach. John had great fun playing catch with his father.

John was all smiles that evening as he was being tucked into bed. He said it was the "best birthday ever" because he had spent the whole day with his parents. John is **joyful** because he finds things to be happy about in all situations.

What is one way you can practice being <u>joyful</u>?

Forgiving

Fred is <u>forgiving</u>.

Fred lives on a ranch where his family raises horses. The last horses purchased by his family were wild, and it took patience to earn their trust.

One day a startled horse kicked Fred, breaking his rib. It was very painful, and Fred had to stay away from the horses a while to heal.

When Fred began training the horses again, he was patient and **forgiving** of the one that kicked him. Fred knew the horse had been very frightened when it was captured in the wild and brought to his ranch.

What is one way you can practice being <u>forgiving</u>?

Patient

Pierre is <u>patient</u>.

Pierre was six years old when his brother was born, and many things began to change. Pierre's mother now spent a lot of time feeding and bathing his baby brother, and changing his diaper.

Pierre quickly told his parents whenever he heard the baby wake and cry. He always waited while his mother took care of the baby. Pierre was **patient** because he made sure the baby was OK before he asked for something he wanted.

Since Pierre was patient, his mother had an easier time looking after both boys. Pierre and his brother became great friends as they grew up.

What is one way you can practice being <u>patient</u>?

Humble

Heidi is <u>humble</u>.

Heidi and three friends formed a spelling bee team. They practiced together, spelling a long list of words. Her teammates had trouble with some of the words, but Heidi studied very hard until she was sure she knew them all.

When the team won first place in the spelling bee, they were all very excited, and Heidi's friends thanked her. However, she said she could not have done so well without the help of her teammates, who helped her study. Heidi is **humble** because she shared the credit for her team's success.

What is one way you can practice being <u>humble</u>?

Grateful

Gail is <u>grateful</u>.

Gail and her father both enjoy collecting rocks. When her father travels for work, he usually brings Gail a new rock for her collection. She treasures each rock and is very **grateful** to her father. Because Gail appreciates the gifts, her father enjoys finding more rocks for her.

One day Gail found a new type of rock at a shop. So, Gail used her allowance to buy the special rock for her father. Because her father gave her so many good things, she wanted to give him something special.

Wow! Was her father surprised—and **grateful**, too!

What is one way you can practice being <u>*grateful*</u>*?*

Peaceful

Penny is <u>peaceful</u>.

Penny's school had a fire drill. Many of the kindergarten students were scared by the loud alarm, and didn't know where they were supposed to go.

Penny, who was in the third grade, walked by their room and thought maybe she could help. With the permission of the teachers, she calmly stepped toward the front of the line and asked the younger students to follow her to the nearest exit.

Penny cared about the other children, and was **peaceful** as she led them to safety.

What is one way you can practice being <u>peaceful</u>?

Juliette Garesché Dages helped to found Peace Learning Circles, a non-profit organization that teaches conflict resolution skills to children. She lives in Kenosha, Wisconsin.

R. W. Alley is the illustrator for the popular Abbey Press adult series of Elf-help books, as well as an illustrator and writer of children's books. He lives in Barrington, Rhode Island, with his wife, daughter, and son. See a wide variety of his works at: www.rwalley.com.